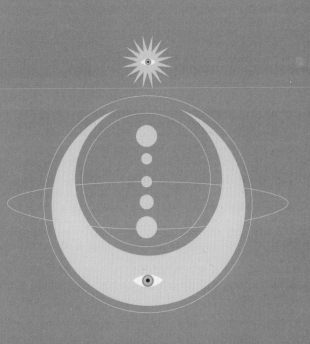

To Gabby Schiavi

VIRGO

A guide to living your best astrological life

STELLA ANDROMEDA

ILLUSTRATED BY EVI O. STUDIO

Hardie Grant

BOOKS

Introduction 7

I.
Get to Know Virgo

Virgo characteristics   31
Physical Virgo   34
How Virgo communicates   37
Virgo careers   38
How Virgo chimes   41
Who loves whom?   44

II.
The Virgo Deep Dive

The Virgo home   55
Self-care   57
Food and cooking   59
How Virgo handles money   61
How Virgo handles the boss   62
What is Virgo like to live with?   65
How to handle a break-up   66
How Virgo wants to be loved   69
Virgo's sex life   72

III.

Give Me More

Your birth chart   76
The Moon effect   80
The 10 planets   83
The four elements   89
Cardinal, fixed and mutable signs   92
The 12 houses   95
The ascendant   101
Saturn return   103
Mercury retrograde   104

Further reading   108
Acknowledgements   109
About the author   111

Introduction

Inscribed on the forecourt of the ancient Greek temple of Apollo at Delphi are the words 'know thyself'. This is one of the 147 Delphic maxims, or rules to live by, attributed to Apollo himself, and was later extended by the philosopher Socrates to the sentence, 'The unexamined life is not worth living.'

People seek a variety of ways of knowing themselves, of coming to terms with life and trying to find ways to understand the challenges of human existence, often through therapy or belief systems like organised religion. These are ways in which we strive to understand the relationships we have with ourselves and others better, seeking out particular tools that enable us to do so.

As far as systems of understanding human nature and experience go, astrology has much to offer through its symbolic use of the constellations of the heavens, the depictions of the zodiac signs, the planets and their energetic effects. Many people find accessing this information and harnessing its potential a useful way of thinking about how to manage their lives more effectively.

What is astrology?

In simple terms, astrology is the study and interpretation of how the planets can influence us, and the world in which we live, through an understanding of their positions at a specific place in time. The practice of astrology relies on a combination of factual knowledge of the characteristics of these positions and their psychological interpretation.

Astrology is less of a belief system and more of a tool for living, from which ancient and established wisdom can be drawn. Any of us can learn to use astrology, not so much for divination or telling the future, but as a guidebook that provides greater insight and a more thoughtful way of approaching life. Timing is very much at the heart of astrology, and knowledge of planetary configurations and their relationship to each other at specific moments in time can assist in helping us with the timing of some of our life choices and decisions.

Knowing when major life shifts can occur – because of particular planetary configurations such as a Saturn return (see page 103) or Mercury retrograde (see page 104) – or what it means to have Venus in your seventh house (see pages 85 and 98), while recognising the specific characteristics of your sign, are all tools that you can use to your advantage. Knowledge is power, and astrology can be a very powerful supplement to approaching life's ups and downs and any relationships we form along the way.

The 12 signs of the zodiac

Each sign of the zodiac has a range of recognisable characteristics, shared by people born under that sign. This is your Sun sign, which you probably already know – and the usual starting point from which we each begin to explore our own astrological paths. Sun sign characteristics can be strongly exhibited in an individual's make-up; however, this is only part of the picture.

Usually, how we appear to others is tempered by the influence of other factors – and these are worth bearing in mind. Your ascendant sign is equally important, as is the positioning of your Moon. You can also look to your opposite sign to see what your Sun sign may need a little more of, to balance its characteristics.

After getting to know your Sun sign in the first part of this book, you might want to dive into the Give Me More section (see pages 74–105) to start to explore all the particulars of your birth chart. These will give you far greater insight into the myriad astrological influences that may play out in your life.

Sun signs

It takes 365 (and a quarter, to be precise) days for the Earth to orbit the Sun and in so doing, the Sun appears to us to spend a month travelling through each sign of the zodiac. Your Sun sign is therefore an indication of the sign that the Sun was travelling through at the time of your birth. Knowing what Sun signs you and your family, friends and lovers are provides you with just the beginning of the insights into character and personality that astrology can help you discover.

On the cusp

For those for whom a birthday falls close to the end of one Sun sign and the beginning of another, it's worth knowing what time you were born. There's no such thing, astrologically, as being 'on the cusp' – because the signs begin at a specific time on a specific date, although this can vary a little year on year. If you are not sure, you'll need to know your birth date, birth time and birth place to work out accurately to which Sun sign you belong. Once you have these, you can consult an astrologer or run your details through an online astrology site program (see page 108) to give you the most accurate birth chart possible.

Taurus

The bull

21 APRIL–20 MAY

Aries

The ram

21 MARCH–20 APRIL

Astrologically the first sign of the zodiac, Aries appears alongside the vernal (or spring) equinox. A cardinal fire sign, depicted by the ram, it is the sign of beginnings and ruled by planet Mars, which represents a dynamic ability to meet challenges energetically and creatively. Its opposite sign is airy Libra.

Grounded, sensual and appreciative of bodily pleasures, Taurus is a fixed earth sign endowed by its ruling planet Venus with grace and a love of beauty, despite its depiction as a bull. Generally characterised by an easy and uncomplicated, if occasionally stubborn, approach to life, Taurus' opposite sign is watery Scorpio.

Gemini

The twins

✦

21 MAY–20 JUNE

A mutable air sign symbolised by
the twins, Gemini tends to see both
sides of an argument, its speedy
intellect influenced by its ruling
planet Mercury. Tending to fight
shy of commitment, this sign also
epitomises a certain youthfulness
of attitude. Its opposite sign is
fiery Sagittarius.

Cancer

The crab

✦

21 JUNE–21 JULY

Depicted by the crab and the
tenacity of its claws, Cancer is a
cardinal water sign, emotional and
intuitive, its sensitivity protected
by its shell. Ruled by the maternal
Moon, the shell also represents the
security of home, to which Cancer
is committed. Its opposite sign is
earthy Capricorn.

Leo

The lion

★

22 JULY–21 AUGUST

A fixed fire sign, ruled by the Sun, Leo loves to shine and is an idealist at heart, positive and generous to a fault. Depicted by the lion, Leo can roar with pride and be confident and uncompromising, with a great faith and trust in humanity. Its opposite sign is airy Aquarius.

Virgo

The virgin

★

22 AUGUST–21 SEPTEMBER

Traditionally represented as a maiden or virgin, this mutable earth sign is observant, detail oriented and tends towards self-sufficiency. Ruled by Mercury, Virgos benefit from a sharp intellect that can be self-critical, while often being very health conscious. Its opposite sign is watery Pisces.

Scorpio

The scorpion

★

22 OCTOBER–21 NOVEMBER

Given to intense feelings, as befits a fixed water sign, Scorpio is depicted by the scorpion – linking it to the rebirth that follows death – and is ruled by both Pluto and Mars. With a strong spirituality and deep emotions, Scorpio needs security to transform its strength. Its opposite sign is earthy Taurus.

Libra

The scales

★

22 SEPTEMBER–21 OCTOBER

A cardinal air sign, ruled by Venus, Libra is all about beauty, balance (as depicted by the scales) and harmony in its rather romanticised, ideal world. With a strong aesthetic sense, Libra can be both arty and crafty, but also likes fairness and can be very diplomatic. Its opposite sign is fiery Aries.

Sagittarius

The archer

★

22 NOVEMBER–21 DECEMBER

Depicted by the archer, Sagittarius is a mutable fire sign that's all about travel and adventure, in body or mind, and is very direct in approach. Ruled by the benevolent Jupiter, Sagittarius is optimistic with lots of ideas; liking a free rein, but with a tendency to generalise. Its opposite sign is airy Gemini.

Capricorn

The goat

★

22 DECEMBER–20 JANUARY

Ruled by Saturn, Capricorn is a cardinal earth sign associated with hard work and depicted by the sure-footed and sometimes playful goat. Trustworthy and unafraid of commitment, Capricorn is often very self-sufficient and has the discipline for the freelance working life. Its opposite sign is the watery Cancer.

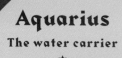

Aquarius
The water carrier

✳

21 JANUARY–19 FEBRUARY

Confusingly, given its depiction
by the water carrier, Aquarius
is a fixed air sign ruled by the
unpredictable Uranus, sweeping
away old ideas with innovative
thinking. Tolerant, open-minded
and all about humanity, its vision
is social with a conscience. Its
opposite sign is fiery Leo.

Pisces
The fish

✳

20 FEBRUARY–20 MARCH

Acutely responsive to its
surroundings, Pisces is a mutable
water sign depicted by two fish,
swimming in opposite directions,
sometimes confusing fantasy with
reality. Ruled by Neptune, its
world is fluid, imaginative and
empathetic, often picking up on
the moods of others. Its opposite
sign is earthy Virgo.

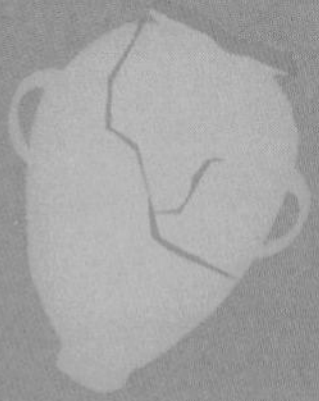

Know

Virgo

The sign the Sun
was travelling in at the
time you were born is the
ultimate starting point
in exploring your character
and personality through
the zodiac.

Mutable earth sign depicted
by the chaste corn-maiden.

Ruled by Mercury, the
planet associated with the
messenger of the gods, linked
to communication and travel.

OPPOSITE SIGN

Pisces

STATEMENT OF SELF

'I analyse.'

Lucky colour

Blue or orange, either colour blocked, or subtly used in a classic pin-stripe detail that's so characteristic of Virgo's style. Wear these colours and connect with your Virgo energy when you need a psychological boost and additional courage, choosing accessories – shoes, gloves, socks, hat or even underwear – if you don't have other clothes in these colours.

Lucky day

Wednesday. The middle of the working week for most of us, this links to the old-English deity Woden, so it's actually Woden's day *(Wōdnesdæg)*. Woden's Roman equivalent is the Mercury of Gemini influence, which we see more obviously in the French for Wednesday, *Mercredi*.

Lucky gem

The blue sapphire is Virgo's precious stone, which evokes a peaceful mind and is said to protect, especially while travelling. Princess Diana's intense, velvety blue Ceylon sapphire engagement ring, now worn by Kate Middleton, is one of the most famous examples of Virgo's luckiest gem.

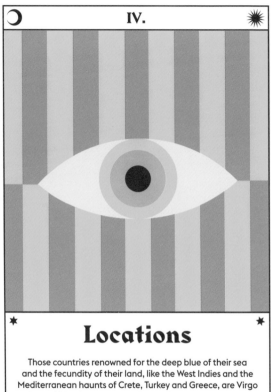

IV.

Locations

Those countries renowned for the deep blue of their sea and the fecundity of their land, like the West Indies and the Mediterranean haunts of Crete, Turkey and Greece, are Virgo places. Cities that resonate with this Sun sign include Paris, Maidstone, Boston, Jerusalem and Brindisi.

Holidays

Activity holidays can be a favourite for Virgo, so skiing
in the French Alps might be an option, or a guided hiking trip
along the Yosemite Falls trail, or a yoga holiday in Greece.
Any of these would allow Virgo to connect with their
body while also relaxing their busy mind.

Flowers

The pansy, derived from the French *pensée*, for thought, and otherwise known as viola or heartsease, to heal the heartache of love. The dark blue or purple varieties also chime with Virgo's lucky colour.

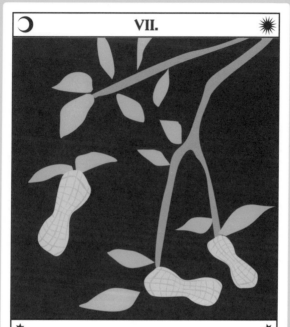

Trees

The hazel, walnut, almond and other nut-bearing trees, including the mighty oak with its acorn, are aligned to Virgo. This species represents the ability to utilise intense energy from which great trees can grow up from their deep roots below, not unlike the accomplishments of this mutable but earthy sign.

Pets

A dog, and probably one of the smaller, short-haired breeds, is likely to appeal to routine-oriented Virgo, who will love to attend obedience classes and go on walks with their pet. You can be sure that Virgo will not only lavish great care on their pooch, they will also train it really well.

Parties

Virgos love to throw a party! It's likely to be one that's perfect in its style, guests, menu and decorations, because they are all about the detail, and can be relied upon to get it right, down to the last beautiful hand-calligraphed place setting. Only then might Virgo reach for a drink. Something like a Cherry Thyme Cocktail, or a long draught of craft beer, straight from the corn maiden's hops.

Virgo characteristics

Traditionally represented by the virgin, or chaste corn-maiden, there is something of a paradox about Virgo, because this sign is also linked to the creative and fertile Earth Mother. We could say Virgo is all about abundance, but abundance that is often kept in check. That reserve is all part of their *modus operandi*, and keeping something back means that they are always prepared, like the proverbial boy scout. Need a piece of string or a clean pair of socks? Virgo won't let you down.

There's something very fastidious, analytical and detail-oriented about Virgo, too, as they go about making their lists, finessing their spreadsheets and ensuring things happen to schedule. They are a wonderful employee as they never drop the ball, but this can sometimes be to their own detriment, as they can get stuck as a 'handmaiden' rather than a boss, which is a shame, as they are very good at running their own show, too.

Sometimes accused of being rather boring, Virgo is also genuinely capable of fun (once the chores are done!) and as an earth sign operates happily on a physical, sensual level. They are very comfortable in their bodies, well co-ordinated and deft in movement, even while operating so well in their minds, thanks to the influence of their ruling planet, Mercury, which is all about intelligent communication.

They are practical but discriminating, conscientious but warm, with a unique combination of opposites that can sometimes clash and cause them stress, because they never, ever want to let anyone down. Again, there may be something of a paradox at first glance, as their desks (and handbags) can look untidy, but this is to do with their innate creativity, on which their practical side can usefully deliver. And, generally, Virgo will know where everything is, because they've kept a record in their very self-sufficient head, for a start.

For Virgo, who can be wonderfully objective, criticism is seldom personal and usually helpfully meant, and they can be just as self-critical, cutting themselves even less slack than they allow others. Spontaneity isn't exactly their first instinct and they tend to hold back, trying too hard sometimes to get things right rather than get them done. All this conscientiousness can spill over into an obsession with making sure everything is perfect, but luckily most Virgos have a good dose of realism that protects them from the worst of their own intentions.

TEMPERING
THE EARTH

The key characteristics of any
Sun sign can be balanced out
(or sometimes reinforced) by the
characteristics of other signs in the
same birth chart, particularly those
of the ascendant and the Moon.
So if someone doesn't appear to
be typical of their Sun sign, that's
why. However, those nascent Virgo
aspects will always be there as
a key influence, informing an
individual's approach to life.

Physical
Virgo

Tidy and well co-ordinated, you're unlikely to find Virgo with a grubby collar or a button missing from their jacket: they are the sign most likely to dress appropriately, whether this is for a rave or a job interview. They know how to present themselves whatever the circumstances – knowing that because first impressions count, it's only sensible to do so. That sort of attention to detail includes their body language, too, and for an earth sign ruled by the planet of communication, this is essential. So Virgos know the value of the direct look, firm handshake and open smile, and it's genuine.

Health

Virgo rules the nervous system and the intestines; and, as the two are linked in the gut, this is where they may show a physical response to stress. What in one person could be a susceptibility to bloating, may be irritable bowel syndrome in another, but their interest in the body and health means that Virgos generally understand how to take responsibility and care for themselves. Because of this, they can sometimes seem to be picky about food, but this is only because they know what doesn't agree with them and what to avoid.

Exercise

Like pretty much everything else they do, the Virgo commitment to their body means that they tend to exercise regularly and do so in a relatively disciplined fashion. They know that exercise also helps alleviate the psychological stress that can give rise to gut problems, and so a daily 15-minute home stretch and aerobics session, or a jog to work, is often how many Virgos choose to start their day.

How Virgo communicates

Analytical (sometimes to a fault) Virgo likes nothing better than good conversation about something of substance, that can be picked apart and put back together again. With a tendency to ask a lot of questions, this also serves to deflect attention from themselves: very often people realise that they have had a long conversation in which they've revealed a lot of themselves but learned nothing of their Virgo friend. This self-reserve isn't immediately obvious to others, but it can mark Virgo out as rather a private person, willing to talk others through their problems, but revealing little of their own. With friends who are sensitive to this, it's fine, but otherwise there's a tendency for Virgos to feel that they don't matter. In order to realise that they do, they will have to learn to open up a little and remember that communication is a two-way street with those they trust.

Virgo careers

Working in the health profession often suits Virgo well, as it combines an interest in the body and how it works, with that slightly detached compassion that makes for a skilled doctor or nurse. Other health-related professions, like a a pharmacist, nutritionist, aromatherapist or physiotherapist can also be a really satisfying way of linking to a Virgo commitment to promoting health. That interest could extend into analysing and supporting the health of the mind in psychology or psychoanalysis, because the mind and what makes other people tick is often fascinating to Virgo.

An analytical mind and a head for figures could make accountancy, working as a statistician or a market analyst, satisfying careers for Virgo, too. Their exceptional eye for detail, along with a precise way with words, might lend itself to book editing, as editing in general suits a good memory and thoughtful application of intelligence. In writing, these skills combined with the art of criticism – whether books, film or sport – could easily appeal to those with a talent for objective and thoughtful analysis of ideas.

How Virgo chimes

Virgo is as conscientious about their relationships as anything else. The friend who never forgets your birthday? Probably Virgo. The card arrives on time and any gift is well chosen and exquisitely wrapped. There is a thoughtfulness and practicality about Virgo that creates a reassuring aura, and their desire to make order out of chaos means they seldom let people down. The depiction of a chaste virgin belies an earthy sensuality, but their reserve means that they tend to handle feelings carefully and are unlikely to splurge emotionally. Virgos need intellectual as well as emotional stimulation, but a tendency to overthink can get in the way of just saying what they feel, and means that they can sometimes be judged as a little chilly, which can hurt them.

The Virgo woman

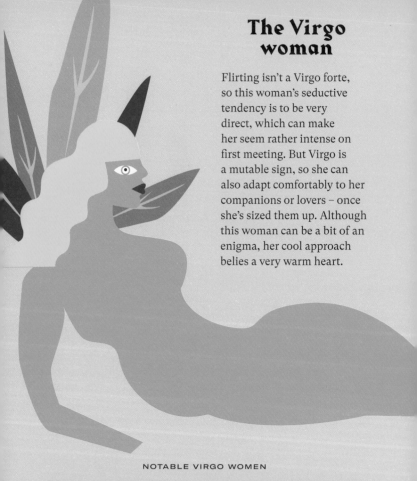

Flirting isn't a Virgo forte, so this woman's seductive tendency is to be very direct, which can make her seem rather intense on first meeting. But Virgo is a mutable sign, so she can also adapt comfortably to her companions or lovers – once she's sized them up. Although this woman can be a bit of an enigma, her cool approach belies a very warm heart.

NOTABLE VIRGO WOMEN

Enigmatic Greta Garbo with her aloof beauty and desire to be alone; Mother Theresa; actresses Lauren Bacall, Jennifer Hudson and Selma Hayek; and Queen Elizabeth I (the original Virgin Queen) all share Virgo traits of intelligence, dedication, discrimination and the sense that feelings are often deeply but secretively held. Underneath that cool exterior, there's deep passion.

The Virgo man

On first meeting, it would be easy to think that this man is the strong silent type but he's just getting the measure of the situation. Once he's got you in his sights, he is genuine and will tend to show his love in practical ways – like putting up a bookshelf. But he doesn't wear his heart on his sleeve, so it's not always easy to tell he has a sensitive soul.

Who love

s whom?

Virgo & Aries

There's an immediate tension here between prudent Virgo and impulsive Aries that can create an emotional uneasiness between them, even when there's a strong intellectual connection and attraction.

Virgo & Taurus

Between these two earth signs lies a nice harmony as both have a practical inclination but also a sensual streak. Creating a secure future together means creating a lovely home, on which they both agree and can easily live happily ever after.

Virgo & Gemini

Their intellectual approach to life means there's an immediate affinity, but Virgo tends to find Gemini's airiness unpredictable, while Virgo's earthy nature is a bit too stuck in the mud. Without a lot of thought, this relationship can be tricky.

Virgo & Cancer

This is a happy, loving combination, as both recognise each other's hidden sensuality, and make a good match in their need for domestic harmony. Virgo's protective streak suits affectionate Cancer, who also makes Virgo feel secure.

Virgo & Leo

Leo's exuberance can be too much for Virgo's reserved nature, both in the bedroom and the domestic purse. Guarding against extravagance irritates Leo and temperamentally they are ill-suited unless they proceed with care.

Virgo & Virgo

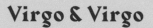

With so much in common, it can be a relief for Virgo to fall in love with Virgo and they will talk as much as anything else in the bedroom. They are so well and happily matched that the only fly in the ointment may be a jostling for first place.

Virgo &
Scorpio

Even while they admire each other's minds, the highly logical nature of Virgo makes it difficult to accept Scorpio's more imaginative ways, although there is a deep appreciation for their loyalty which can help override any conflict.

Virgo & Libra

Virgo's natural reserve is tricky for Libra to understand and they can interpret this as a rebuff, even when it's not the case, while Virgo feels that Libra's love of the good things in life is too frivolous. This combination needs careful handling.

Virgo &
Sagittarius

The reckless traveller is difficult for hard-working Virgo to understand, and troubling to their need to put down roots. Even with a closely aligned intellect, clashes are likely to be deep-seated, considering their different temperaments.

Virgo & Aquarius

Although of similar intellectual approach, each can be rather remote and together this gets exaggerated. Virgo's practical ambitions are not well matched by Aquarius' more cerebral engagement with life, which can create problems.

Virgo & Pisces

There may be too many opposites to overcome between these two, as Virgo's more precise ways tend to clash with Pisces all-encompassing view of life's possibilities, while their dreaminess can irritate Virgo's practicality.

Virgo & Capricorn

There's an immediate harmony between the happy diligence of these two earth signs. They like and respect each other's purposeful approach to life and love, and intuitively they recognise a need for approval and mutual achievement.

Virgo love-o-meter

Least compatible

Sagittarius   Aries   Pisces   Leo   Aquarius   Libra

Most compatible

Gemini   Scorpio   Capricorn   Cancer   Taurus   Virgo

The Virgo

II.

Deep Dive

In this section, dive deeper into the ways in which your Sun sign might be driving you or holding you back, and start to think about how you might use this knowledge to inform your path.

The Virgo home

The Virgo home is usually very attractive and welcoming, with comfortable furniture and simple décor, because Virgo enjoys and takes pleasure in creating a home that is easy to live in, and is often happily able to put up shelves, paint walls or make curtains very efficiently. In fact, this ability may extend to an artistic talent, featuring beautifully crafted carpentry, hand-painted kitchen tiles, silk-screened prints, paintings or other artistic pieces. For Virgo, beauty in an object also comes from its usefulness and the way it sits pleasingly with those around it, so there is often a style and harmony in their home that can be very modern, with clean lines and lovely combinations of materials, textures and colours.

Gardening can be a particular Virgo pleasure, and the garden may be seen as an extension of their living space, as carefully thought out and designed as any other room in the house. Medicinal plants and herbs might feature, too, even if only in window boxes.

TOP TIPS FOR
VIRGO SELF-CARE

* Book a weekend retreat to learn mindfulness meditation.

* Sleep more! Use that famous Virgo discipline to go to bed on time.

* Keep hydrated to help balance the body's internal environment.

Self-care

For all their commitment to health, Virgo tends to focus on others rather than themselves and can sometimes neglect their own self-care. It should be prioritised, though, as Virgo is susceptible to perfectionism and consequently burning the candle at both ends. Overwork and insisting on doing everything themselves can be a disastrous combination and take its toll on Virgo's health. One of the ways to improve self-care for Virgo might be to buddy up and factor in relaxation and exercise activities with a friend, achieving two things at once: helping them and helping themselves.

Stress management is also an important aspect for Virgo. The effects of stress can be reduced through a combination of mindful and physical approaches, and for Virgo this should be made a priority. Fatigue, too, is so often ignored by workaholic types that its symptoms can go unrecognised for what they are, and easily misinterpreted by Virgo who also has an inclination towards hypochondria. They need to remind themselves that a pounding heart rate can be a direct consequence of the physical exhaustion caused by lack of sleep and isn't necessarily a sign of something more serious.

WHAT TO KEEP
IN THE VIRGO
PANTRY

* Home-made green
  tomato chutney.

* Rice noodles.

* Organic, gluten-free tamari
  soy sauce.

Food
and
cooking

Not so much faddy as particular, Virgos enjoy cooking and preparing simple meals with high-quality ingredients. For them, food supports their body, it's the fuel it runs on, so they are careful about what they eat, often choosing healthy food and ingredients that support their digestive system. Wholegrains, seeds, nuts, fresh and locally produced (often home-grown) vegetables, free-range eggs, organic meat and fish from sustainable stock, are all high on Virgo's shopping list. They may even opt for a macrobiotic or vegan diet.

Virgos take care over their cooking and enjoy meticulous preparation, priding themselves on their knowledge and skill. Along with being nutritiously balanced, their dishes always look perfect. Virgos also hate waste, so their gourmet skills often extend to getting creative with tasty leftovers. That delicious shepherd's pie or moussaka? It's made of the home-minced lamb left over from Sunday roast. Nothing's ever wasted.

TOP TIPS FOR VIRGO'S MONEY

★ Have a small savings fund allocated *just* for having fun.

★ Consulting financial experts is a good call; even Virgos don't know it all.

★ Investing in bricks and mortar is always appealing to earth signs, but explore other options.

How Virgo handles money

Because they tend to be hard-working and cautious, any risk Virgo takes with money is usually a well-researched and calculated one. There are no rash investments, no interest in cryptic currencies or pyramid schemes, and what financial speculation is indulged in will only happen after sounding out extensive advice. Virgo is likely to have thought about a retirement pension in their twenties and will consider work partly on the basis of its financial security. They invest for the long haul rather than for a fast buck and, as a result, are often very financially savvy. It is not something that worries them, because they always check the small print. Because of this approach, gambling makes no sense to them at all because there is no guarantee of any return: the odds of winning the lottery are so unfeasible, Virgos won't waste their money. The closest they'll get to a punt is a small bet on a horse named after their grandmother on Derby day, and that's it.

How Virgo handles the boss

Many Virgos at work feel frustrated at the way their boss works, thinking they could probably do the job better. Even if this were true, it's better not to let on, because in spite of Virgo efficiency there's probably more to someone else's job than meets the eye. Instead, Virgos may need to learn to *tactfully* suggest other ways of doing things, probably backed up with some of their meticulous research to prove their point. It's just as well that this sign is ruled by the planet of communication, because this can help Virgo find a way to be diplomatic. Even then, it's impossible to predict how a boss might respond, so learning to bite their tongue on occasion can sometimes be the most effective approach.

However, most bosses are generally so appreciative of Virgo's competence and attention to detail, there is often a tendency to dump an increasingly heavy workload on them, as they adapt willingly to take the strain. Priding themselves on being able to manage everything that's thrown at them, many Virgos exceed the requirements of their job spec, and need to guard against this and ensure they get the relevant acknowledgement and remuneration for what they do.

TOP TIPS TO HANDLE THE BOSS

* Always give feedback and criticism with a solution-based focus.

* Be very clear on when the demands of the job exceed its original spec.

* Consider being your own boss: Virgos love being completely in control.

TOP TIPS FOR AN EASIER LIFE

★ A domestic chores rota will help everyone's organisation.

★ Wait to be asked for advice before you give it.

★ You may be better than everyone else at stacking the dishwasher, but remember it's not a dealbreaker.

What is Virgo like to live with?

That practicality and thoughtfulness they're famous for should make Virgo a dream housemate, right? Think again, because in some cases, that organisational side of Virgo isn't always evident in their living environment. Their minds might be tidy, they might always show up neatly dressed, the bathtub might be pristine and there's no mouldy food in the fridge, but their room may be as chaotic as the proverbial teenager's. While order is important in some areas, sentimentality can win the day in others, and throwing things out isn't always the Virgo way, which can lead to a lot of personal clutter.

Where they live and who they live with is definitely important to Virgo, but they may not be very expressive about this. That reserved nature means they don't always say how much their housemate or partner means to them, but they'll be first to show their commitment in deeds. They'll also be up for late-night discussions on both national politics or the latest TV celebrity gossip, analysing the human behaviour of both, and will happily hear out a housemate on an emotional problem through to the wee small hours.

How to handle a break-up

Virgo is not a clingy sign and can tend to appear rather stoic about break-ups. Despite this, they are often stunned when they have to experience a relationship falling apart, because, like everything else in life, they believe they should have been able to fix it. They also have a tendency to rationalise and bury their feelings to protect themselves, so it's not always obvious how hurt they are. If they've instigated the break up, Virgo will not do so without very good reason – but this may be more obvious to them than to their ex.

Under pressure, the Virgo instinct is to control the situation – whichever side is doing the breaking up – which can actually make things worse. Better to gracefully let things go.

TOP TIPS FOR
AN EASIER BREAK-UP

* Stop analysing: remember the good bits and forget the rest.

* Although it doesn't come easily, confide in a friend.

* Remember it's not always possible to 'think' things better.

How Virgo wants to be loved

The self-restraint typical of many Virgos can make it difficult for them to ask for the love and affection they need, but they are capable of very deep, grounded love and this is the bare minimum of what they expect in return. Consequently, Virgo can feel hurt when their gentle reserve or practical attitude to love gets misinterpreted as a dismissal, although they're unlikely to show it. It's only when Virgo feels truly loved that they feel secure enough to let go of their defensive behaviour, become less inhibited and more passionate, and reveal their vulnerable side. It's not always easy, though: many a would-be lover has feared getting it wrong or being criticised by Virgo, making it difficult to make the first move. Virgo actually hates to hurt other people's feelings and doesn't always realise they are doing so, purely because they are so damned logical.

Getting past this first hurdle takes patience on behalf of any would-be lover.

Another reason it takes Virgo a long time to return love completely is because they have to consider all the reasons, evidence and hard facts that might mean this person isn't Mr or Miss Right (and they don't want to waste their time on Mr or Miss Wrong). Because of this, they can have a tendency to be very discriminating, if not picky, with a checklist of requirements that can look superficial to others – but is just due diligence to Virgo! Wear the wrong socks and you may not merit consideration, regardless of the fact that they adore you.

When this Virgo inclination for thinking things through turns into overthinking, they can be their own worst enemy. It's then that their hyper-logical approach can get in the way of the need for Virgo to occasionally compromise to get what they want – which is to be loved completely and passionately by someone who sees beyond their self-imposed restrictions. However, because they are also a highly adaptable sign, with the right person they can always be persuaded to change.

TOP TIPS FOR LOVING VIRGO

★ Have patience: that distance may be masking insecurity, not lack of interest.

★ Deeds matter as much as words to cut through Virgo reserve.

★ Take some time; romance matters hugely at the start.

Virgo's sex life

As you'd expect from a sign that enjoys planning events, lovers can feel very cherished by Virgo's attention to detail. Yes, Virgo can do spontaneous and uninhibited because they are also an adaptable sign, but they do like to stage-manage things a bit because, when pleasure's at stake, it's worth taking a little trouble, surely? But there's a big difference between taking a little trouble and giving stage directions in bed and sometimes Virgo just has to do the diplomatic thing and keep quiet.

The instinct to give 100 per cent to their partner makes Virgo a sensitive lover, as long as they can resist mentally checking all is going well and just abandon themselves to the moment. Virgo also needs to remember that receiving pleasure is as important as giving when it comes to making love, and the bedroom is one place where perfection *really* doesn't matter because it's all about trust and sharing and creating something special between the two people in the room and them alone. But the more secure Virgo feels in a relationship, the more easily they relax in the bedroom, and that's when the erotic magic can really happen.

Give

III.

Me More

Your Sun sign never shows you the whole picture. In this section, learn how to read the nuances of your birth chart and discover a whole new level of astrological insight.

Your birth chart

Your birth chart is a snapshot of a particular moment, in a particular place, at the precise moment of your birth and is therefore completely individual to you. It's like a blueprint, a map, a statement of occurrence, spelling out possible traits and influences – but it isn't your destiny. It is just a symbolic tool to which you can refer, based on the position of the planets at the time of your birth. If you can't get to an astrologer, these days anyone can get their birth chart prepared in minutes online (see page 108 for a list of websites and apps that will do it for you). Even if you don't know your exact time of birth, just knowing the date and place of birth can create the beginnings of a useful template.

Remember, nothing is intrinsically good or bad in astrology and there is no explicit timing or forecasting: it's more a question of influences and how these might play out positively or negatively. And if we have some insight, and some tools with which to approach, see or interpret our circumstances and surroundings, this gives us something to work with.

When you are reading your birth chart, it's useful to first understand all the tools of astrology available to you; not only the astrological signs and what they represent, but also the 10 planets referred to in astrology and their individual characteristics, along with the 12 houses and what they mean. Individually, these tools of astrology are of passing interest, but when you start to see how they might sit in juxtaposition to each other, then the bigger picture becomes more accessible and we begin to gain insights that can be useful to us.

Broadly speaking, each of the planets suggests a different type of energy, the astrological signs propose the various ways in which that energy might be expressed, while the houses represent areas of experience in which this expression might operate.

Next to bring into the picture are the positions of the signs at four key points: the ascendant, or rising sign, and its opposite, the descendant; and the midheaven and its opposite, the IC, not to mention the different aspects created by congregations of signs and planets.

It is now possible to see how subtle the reading of a birth chart might be and how it is infinite in its variety, and highly specific to an individual. With this information, and a working understanding of the symbolic meaning and influences of the signs, planets and houses of your unique astrological profile, you can begin to use these tools to help with decision-making and other aspects of life.

Reading your chart

If you have your birth chart prepared, either by hand or via an online program, you will see a circle divided into 12 segments, with information clustered at various points indicating the position of each zodiac sign, in which segment it appears and at what degree. Irrespective of the features that are relevant to the individual, each chart follows the same pattern when it comes to interpretation.

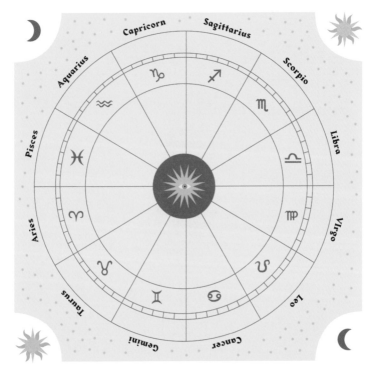

Virgo

Given the time of birth, the place of birth and the position of the planets at that moment, the birth chart, sometimes called a natal horoscope, is drawn up.

If you consider the chart as a clock face, the first house (see pages 95–99 for the astrological houses) begins at the 9, and it is from this point that, travelling anti-clockwise the chart is read from the first house, through the 12 segments of the chart to the twelfth.

The beginning point, the 9, is also the point at which the Sun rises on your life, giving you your ascendant, or rising sign, and opposite to this, at the 3 of the clock face, is your descendant sign. The midheaven point of your chart, the MC, is at 12, and its opposite, the IC, at 6 (see pages 101–102).

Understanding the significance of the characteristics of the astrological signs and the planets, their particular energies, their placements and their aspects to each other can be helpful in understanding ourselves and our relationships with others. In day-to-day life, too, the changing configuration of planets and their effects are much more easily understood with a basic knowledge of astrology, as are the recurring patterns that can sometimes strengthen and sometimes delay opportunities and possibilities. Working with, rather than against, these trends can make life more manageable and, in the last resort, more successful.

The Moon effect

If your Sun sign represents your consciousness, your life force and your individual will, then the Moon represents that side of your personality that you tend to keep rather secret or hidden. This is the realm of instinct, intuition, creativity and the unconscious, which can take you places emotionally that are sometimes hard to understand. This is what brings great subtlety and nuance to a person, way beyond just their Sun sign. So you may have your Sun in Virgo, and all that means, but this might be countered by a mystical and imaginative Moon in Pisces; or you may have your Sun in open-hearted Leo, but a Moon in Aquarius with all its rebellious, emotional detachment.

Phases of the Moon

The Moon orbits the Earth, taking roughly 28 days to do so. How much of the Moon we see is determined by how much of the Sun's light it reflects, giving us the impression that it waxes, or grows, and wanes. When the Moon is new, to us, only a sliver of it is illuminated. As it waxes, it reflects more light and moves from a crescent, to a waxing crescent to a first quarter; then it moves to a waxing gibbous Moon, to a full Moon. Then the Moon begins to wane through a waning gibbous, to a last quarter, and then the cycle begins again. All of this occurs over four weeks. When we have two full Moons in any one calendar month, the second is called a blue Moon.

Each month the Moon also moves through an astrological sign, as we know from our personal birth charts. This, too, will yield information – a Moon in Scorpio can have a very different effect to one in Capricorn – and depending on our personal charts, this can have a shifting influence each month. For example, if the Moon in your birth chart is in Virgo, then when the actual Moon moves into Virgo, this will have an additional influence. Read the characteristics of the signs for further information (see pages 12–17).

The Moon's cycle has an energetic effect, which we can see quite easily on the ocean tides. Astrologically, because the Moon is both a fertility symbol and attuned to our deeper psychological side, we can use this to focus more profoundly and creatively on aspects of life that are important to us.

Eclipses

Generally speaking, an eclipse covers up and prevents light being shed on a situation. Astrologically speaking, this will depend on where the Sun or Moon is positioned in relation to other planets at the time of an eclipse. So if a solar eclipse is in Gemini, there will be a Geminian influence or an influence on Geminis.

Hiding, or shedding, light on an area of our lives is an invitation to pay attention to it. Eclipses are generally about beginnings or endings, which is why our ancestors saw them as portents, important signs to be taken notice of. As it is possible to know when an eclipse is forthcoming, these are charted astronomically; consequently, their astrological significance can be assessed and acted upon ahead of time.

The 10 planets

For the purpose of astrology (but not for astronomy, because the Sun is really a star) we talk about 10 planets, and each astrological sign has a ruling planet, with Mercury, Venus and Mars each being assigned two. The characteristics of each planet describe those influences that can affect signs, all of which information feeds into the interpretation of a birth chart.

The Moon

This sign is an opposing principle to the Sun, forming a pair, and it represents the feminine, symbolising containment and receptivity, how we react most instinctively and with feeling.

Rules the sign of Cancer.

The Sun

The Sun represents the masculine, and is seen as the energy that sparks life, which suggests a paternal energy in our birth chart. It also symbolises our self or essential being, and our purpose.

Rules the sign of Leo.

Mercury

Mercury is the planet of communication and symbolises our urge to make sense of, understand and communicate our thoughts through words.

Rules the signs of Gemini and Virgo.

Venus

The planet of love is all about attraction, connection and pleasure and in a female chart it symbolises her style of femininity, while in a male chart it represents his ideal partner.

Rules the signs of Taurus and Libra.

Mars

This planet symbolises pure energy (Mars was, after all, the god of War) but it also tells you in which areas you're most likely to be assertive, aggressive or to take risks.

Rules the signs of Aries and Scorpio.

Saturn

Saturn is sometimes called the wise teacher or taskmaster of astrology, symbolising lessons learnt and limitations, showing us the value of determination, tenacity and resilience.

Rules the sign of Capricorn.

Jupiter

The planet Jupiter is the largest in our solar system and symbolises bounty and benevolence, all that is expansive and jovial. Like the sign it rules, it's also about moving away from the home on journeys and exploration.

Rules the sign of Sagittarius.

Uranus

This planet symbolises the unexpected, new ideas and innovation, and the urge to tear down the old and usher in the new. The downside can mark an inability to fit in and consequently the feeling of being an outsider.

Rules the sign of Aquarius.

Pluto

Aligned to Hades (*Pluto* in Latin), the god of the underworld or death, the planet exerts a powerful force that lies below the surface and which, in its most negative form, can represent obsessions and compulsive behaviour.

Rules the sign of Scorpio.

Neptune

Linked to the sea, this is about what lies beneath, underwater and too deep to be seen clearly. Sensitive, intuitive and artistic, it also symbolises the capacity to love unconditionally, to forgive and forget.

Rules the sign of Pisces.

The four elements

Further divisions of the 12 astrological signs into the four elements of earth, fire, air and water yield other characteristics. This comes from ancient Greek medicine, where the body was considered to be made up of four bodily fluids or 'humours'. These four humours – blood, yellow bile, black bile and phlegm – corresponded to the four temperaments of sanguine, choleric, melancholic and phlegmatic, to the four seasons of the year, spring, summer, autumn, winter, and the four elements of air, fire, earth and water.

Related to astrology, these symbolic qualities cast further light on characteristics of the different signs. Carl Jung also used them in his psychology, and we still refer to people as earthy, fiery, airy or wet in their approach to life, while sometimes describing people as 'being in their element'. In astrology, those Sun signs that share the same element are said to have an affinity, or an understanding, with each other.

Like all aspects of astrology, there is always a positive and a negative, and a knowledge of any 'shadow side' can be helpful in terms of self-knowledge and what we may need to enhance or balance out, particularly in our dealings with others.

Air

GEMINI ✴ LIBRA ✴ AQUARIUS

The realm of ideas is where these air signs excel. Perceptive and visionary and able to see the big picture, there is a very reflective quality to air signs that helps to vent situations. Too much air, however, can dissipate intentions, so Gemini might be indecisive, Libra has a tendency to sit on the fence, while Aquarius can be very disengaged.

Fire

ARIES ✴ LEO ✴ SAGITTARIUS

There is a warmth and energy to these signs, a positive approach, spontaneity and enthusiasm that can be inspiring and very motivational to others. The downside is that Aries has a tendency to rush in headfirst, Leo can have a need for attention and Sagittarius can tend to talk it up but not deliver.

Earth

TAURUS * VIRGO * CAPRICORN

Characteristically, these signs enjoy sensual pleasure, enjoying food and other physical pleasures, and they like to feel grounded, preferring to base their ideas in facts. The downside is that Taureans can be stubborn, Virgos can be pernickety and Capricorns can veer towards a dogged conservatism.

Water

CANCER * SCORPIO * PISCES

Water signs are very responsive, like the tide ebbing and flowing, and can be very perceptive and intuitive, sometimes uncannily so because of their ability to feel. The downside is – watery enough – a tendency to feel swamped, and then Cancer can be both tenacious and self-protective, Pisces chameleon-like in their attention and Scorpio unpredictable and intense.

Cardinal, fixed and mutable signs

In addition to the 12 signs being divided into four elements, they can also be grouped into three different ways in which their energies may act or react, giving further depth to each sign's particular characteristics.

Cardinal

ARIES ✳ CANCER ✳ LIBRA ✳ CAPRICORN

These are action planets, with an energy that takes the initiative and gets things started. Aries has the vision, Cancer the feelings, Libra the contacts and Capricorn the strategy.

Fixed

TAURUS ✱ LEO ✱ SCORPIO ✱ AQUARIUS

Slower but more determined, these signs work to progress and maintain those initiatives that the cardinal signs have fired up. Taurus offers physical comfort, Leo loyalty, Scorpio emotional support and Aquarius sound advice. You can count on fixed signs, but they tend to resist change.

Mutable

GEMINI ✱ VIRGO ✱ SAGITTARIUS ✱ PISCES

Adaptable and responsive to new ideas, places and people, mutable signs have a unique ability to adjust to their surroundings. Gemini is mentally agile, Virgo is practical and versatile, Sagittarius visualises possibilities and Pisces is responsive to change.

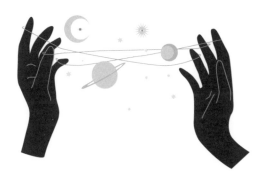

The 12 houses

The birth chart is divided into 12 houses, which represent separate areas and functions of your life. When you are told you have something in a specific house – for example, Libra (balance) in the fifth house (creativity and sex) – it creates a way of interpreting the influences that can arise and are particular to how you might approach an aspect of your life.

Each house relates to a Sun sign, and in this way each is represented by some of the characteristics of that sign, which is said to be its natural ruler.

Three of these houses are considered to be mystical, relating to our interior, psychic world: the fourth (home), eighth (death and regeneration) and twelfth (secrets).

1st House

THE SELF

RULED BY ARIES

This house symbolises the self: you, who you are and how you represent yourself, your likes, dislikes and approach to life. It also represents how you see yourself and what you want in life.

2nd House

POSSESSIONS

RULED BY TAURUS

The second house symbolises your possessions, what you own, including money; how you earn or acquire your income; and your material security and the physical things you take with you as you move through life.

3rd House

COMMUNICATION

RULED BY GEMINI

This house is about communication and mental attitude, primarily how you express yourself. It's also about how you function within your family, and how you travel to school or work, and includes how you think, speak, write and learn.

4th House

HOME

RULED BY CANCER

This house is about your roots and your home or homes, present, past and future, so it includes both your childhood and current domestic set-up. It's also about what home and security represent to you.

5th House

CREATIVITY

RULED BY LEO

Billed as the house of creativity and play, this also includes sex, and relates to the creative urge, the libido, in all its manifestations. It's also about speculation in finance and love, games, fun and affection: affairs of the heart.

6th House

HEALTH

RULED BY VIRGO

This house is related to health: our own physical and emotional health, and how robust it is; but also those we care for, look after or provide support to – from family members to work colleagues.

7th **House**

PARTNERSHIPS

RULED BY LIBRA

The opposite of the first house, this reflects shared goals and intimate partnerships, our choice of life partner and how successful our relationships might be. It also reflects partnerships and adversaries in our professional world.

8th **House**

REGENERATION

RULED BY SCORPIO

For death, read regeneration or spiritual transformation: this house also reflects legacies and what you inherit after death, in personality traits or materially. And because regeneration requires sex, it's also about sex and sexual emotions.

9th **House**

TRAVEL

RULED BY SAGITTARIUS

The house of long-distance travel and exploration, this is also about the broadening of the mind that travel can bring, and how that might express itself. It also reflects the sending out of ideas, which can come about from literary effort or publication.

11th House

FRIENDSHIPS

RULED BY AQUARIUS

The eleventh house is about friendship groups and acquaintances, vision and ideas, and is less about immediate gratification but more concerning longer-term dreams and how these might be realised through our ability to work harmoniously with others.

12th House

SECRETS

RULED BY PISCES

Considered the most spiritual house, it is also the house of the unconscious, of secrets and of what might lie hidden, the metaphorical skeleton in the closet. It also reflects the secret ways we might self-sabotage or imprison our own efforts by not exploring them.

10th House

ASPIRATIONS

RULED BY CAPRICORN

This represents our aspiration and status, how we'd like to be elevated in public standing (or not), our ambitions, image and what we'd like to attain in life, through our own efforts.

The ascendant

Otherwise known as your rising sign, this is the sign of the zodiac that appears at the horizon as dawn breaks on the day of your birth, depending on your location in the world and time of birth. This is why knowing your time of birth is a useful factor in astrology, because your 'rising sign' yields a lot of information about those aspects of your character that are more on show, how you present yourself and how you are seen by others. So, even if you are a Sun Virgo, but have Cancer rising, you may be seen as someone who is maternal, with a noticeable commitment to the domestic life in one way or another. Knowing your own ascendant – or that of another person – will often help explain why there doesn't seem to be such a direct correlation between their personality and their Sun sign.

As long as you know your time of birth and where you were born, working out your ascendant using an online tool or app is very easy (see page 108). Just ask your mum or other family members, or check your birth certificate (in those countries that include a birth time). If the astrological chart were a clock face, the ascendant would be at the 9 o'clock position.

The descendant

The descendant gives an indication of a possible life partner, based on the idea that opposites attract. Once you know your ascendant, the descendant is easy to work out as it is always six signs away: for example, if your ascendant is Virgo, your descendant is Pisces. If the astrological chart were a clock face, the descendant would be at the 3 o'clock position.

The midheaven (MC)

Also included in the birth chart is the position of the midheaven or MC (from the Latin, *medium coeli*, meaning middle of the heavens), which indicates your attitude towards your work, career and professional standing. If the astrological chart were a clock face, the MC would be at the 12 o'clock position.

The IC

Finally, your IC (from the Latin, *imum coeli*, meaning the lowest part of the heavens) indicates your attitude towards your home and family, and is also related to the end of your life. Your IC will be directly opposite your MC: for example, if your MC is Aquarius, your IC is Leo. If the astrological chart were a clock face, the IC would be at the 6 o'clock position.

Saturn return

Saturn is one of the slower-moving planets, taking around 28 years to complete its orbit around the Sun and return to the place it occupied at the time of your birth. This return can last between two to three years and be very noticeable in the period coming up to our thirtieth and sixtieth birthdays, often considered to be significant 'milestone' birthdays.

Because the energy of Saturn is sometimes experienced as demanding, this isn't always an easy period of life. A wise teacher or a hard taskmaster, some consider the Saturn effect as 'cruel to be kind' in the way that many good teachers can be, keeping us on track like a rigorous personal trainer.

Everyone experiences their Saturn return relevant to their circumstances, but it is a good time to take stock, let go of the stuff in your life that no longer serves you and revise your expectations, while being unapologetic about what you would like to include more of in your life. So if you are experiencing or anticipating this life event, embrace and work with it because what you learn now – about yourself, mainly – is worth knowing, however turbulent it might be, and can pay dividends in how you manage the next 28 years!

Mercury retrograde

Even those with little interest in astrology often take notice when the planet Mercury is retrograde. Astrologically, retrogrades are periods when planets are stationary but, as we continue to move forwards, Mercury 'appears' to move backwards. There is a shadow period either side of a retrograde period, when it could be said to be slowing down or speeding up, which can also be a little turbulent. Generally speaking, the advice is not to make any important moves related to communication on a retrograde and, even if a decision is made, know that it's likely to change.

Given that Mercury is the planet of communication, you can immediately see why there are concerns about its retrograde status and its link to communication failures – of the old-fashioned sort when the post office loses a letter, or the more modern technological variety when your computer crashes

– causing problems. Mercury retrograde can also affect travel, with delays in flights or train times, traffic jams or collisions. Mercury also influences personal communications: listening, speaking, being heard (or not), and can cause confusion or arguments. It can also affect more formal agreements, like contracts between buyer and seller.

These retrograde periods occur three to four times a year, lasting for roughly three weeks, with a shadow period either side. The dates in which it happens also mean it occurs within a specific astrological sign. If, for example, it occurs between 25 October and 15 November, its effect would be linked to the characteristics of Scorpio. In addition, those Sun sign Scorpios, or those with Scorpio in significant placements in their chart, may also experience a greater effect.

Mercury retrograde dates are easy to find from an astrological table, or ephemeris, and online. These can be used in order to avoid planning events that might be affected around these times. How Mercury retrograde may affect you more personally requires knowledge of your birth chart and an understanding of its more specific combination of influences with the signs and planets in your chart.

If you are going to weather a Mercury retrograde more easily, be aware that glitches can occur so, to some extent, expect delays and double-check details. Stay positive if postponements occur and consider this period an opportunity to slow down, review or reconsider ideas in your business or your personal life. Use the time to correct mistakes or reshape plans, preparing for when any stuck energy can shift and you can move forward again more smoothly.

Further reading

Astrology Decoded (2013)
by Sue Merlyn Farebrother;
published by Rider

Astrology for Dummies
(2007) by Rae Orion;
published by Wiley Publishing

*Chart Interpretation
Handbook: Guidelines for
Understanding the Essentials
of the Birth Chart* (1990)
by Stephen Arroyo;
published by CRCS
Publications

Jung's Studies in Astrology
(2018) by Liz Greene;
published by RKP

*The Only Astrology
Book You'll Ever Need*
(2012) by Joanne Woolfolk;
published by Taylor Trade

Websites

astro.com

astrologyzone.com

jessicaadams.com

shelleyvonstrunkel.com

Apps

Astrostyle

Co-Star

Susan Miller's Astrology Zone

The Daily Horoscope

The Pattern

Time Passages

Acknowledgements

Particular thanks are due to my trusty team of Taureans. Firstly, to Kate Pollard, Publishing Director at Hardie Grant, for her passion for beautiful books and for commissioning this series. And to Bex Fitzsimons for all her good natured and conscientious editing. And finally to Evi O. Studio, whose illustration and design talents have produced small works of art. With such a star-studded team, these books can only shine and for that, my thanks.

About the author

Stella Andromeda has been studying
astrology for over 30 years, believing that
a knowledge of the constellations of the
skies and their potential for psychological
interpretation can be a useful tool. This
extension of her study into book form makes
modern insights about the ancient wisdom
of the stars easily accessible, sharing her
passion that reflection and self-knowledge
only empowers us in life. With her sun in
Taurus, Aquarius ascendant and Moon
in Cancer, she utilises earth, air and water
to inspire her own astrological journey.

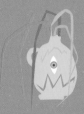

Published in 2019 by Hardie Grant Books,
an imprint of Hardie Grant Publishing

Hardie Grant Books (London)
5th & 6th Floors
52–54 Southwark Street
London SE1 1UN

Hardie Grant Books (Melbourne)
Building 1, 658 Church Street
Richmond, Victoria 3121

hardiegrantbooks.com

All rights reserved. No part of this publication may be reproduced,
stored in a retrieval system or transmitted in any form by any
means, electronic, mechanical, photocopying, recording or
otherwise, without the prior written permission of
the publishers and copyright holders.

The moral rights of the author have been asserted.

Copyright text © Stella Andromeda
Copyright illustrations © Evi O. Studio

British Library Cataloguing-in-Publication Data. A catalogue record
for this book is available from the British Library.

Virgo
ISBN: 9781784882631

10 9 8 7

Publishing Director: Kate Pollard
Junior Editor: Bex Fitzsimons
Art Direction and Illustrations: Evi O. Studio
Editor: Wendy Hobson
Production Controller: Sinead Hering
Colour reproduction by p2d
Printed and bound in China by Leo Paper Products Ltd.